THE ART OF GARNET IFILL
GLIMPSES OF THE SUGAR INDUSTRY

HANSIB PUBLICATIONS

THE ART OF GARNET IFILL

Glimpses of the Sugar Industry

BY DR BRINSLEY SAMAROO

HANSIB

First published in Great Britain in 2003
by Hansib Publications Limited
London: PO Box 34621, London E17 4GL
Hertfordshire: Orchard Road, Royston, Hertfordshire SG8 5HA

With support from the University of the West Indies, St Augustine, Trinidad

Email: info@hansib-books.com. Website: www.hansib-books.com

ISBN 1 870518 76 4

Design and Production by Books of Colour, Hertfordshire, England

Printed and bound by Interprint Limited, Malta

INTRODUCTION

In his Nobel Prize acceptance speech of 1992 Derek Walcott described Antillean art as the "restoration of our shattered histories, our shards of vocabulary, our archipelago becoming a synonym for pieces broken off from the original continent".[1] If this be true then Garnet Ifill must stand out as one of our premier Caribbean artists. From the early fifties of the last century to the present, this photographer has crafted his art like a skilled jeweller.

For some five decades Ifill has been engaged in little but his chosen profession. During this time, he has been able to capture a wide range of themes in a daily changing landscape, on an island which has been home to migrants from Europe, Africa, Asia and the Middle East. Here seasonal changes in climate-from dry to wet season- destroys then recreates the landscape every year. Then there are the *rites de passage* of the ethnicities which offer a panoply of endless variations in colour, rhythm and tone. All of these movements of nature and of people have been painstakingly crafted into Ifill's art.

Those of us who grew up in Trinidad's southern capital of San Fernando can never forget this little man taking up a giant's space as he darted from scene to scene at secondary school speech days and at political meetings during a formative period in the birth of our nation. Those who wanted artful depictions of their weddings, Christenings and sporting activities had no choice but to engage Garnet. Since the 1980's he has added industrial photography to his repertoire which makes his collection perhaps the largest and most varied in Trinidad and Tobago.

In this volume we have drawn from only one of the diverse range of subjects covered

[1] Derek Walcott, *What the twilight says*. New York. 1998. p.69.

by this master artist, namely his portraiture of the sugar industry. The collection starts from the days when the artifices of indentureship were being dismantled and East Indians were moving away from the estates as they sought to forge a space for themselves in the New World. The restoration of that shattered history continues as Ifill takes us through the joys and sorrows of plantation life, the sweet and not so sweet aspects of the transition from indentureship to freedom. The collection is of special significance in view of the fact that this is an industry which is gradually being phased out.

Who is this Garnet Ifill and why did he choose to spend so many of his years recording the plantation-system and its legacy? Ifill is the great-grandson of a Trinidad-born slave, Louisa Kettel who had worked on the sugar estate at Hardbargain in the Williamsville area in South Trinidad. From his grand-mother Sataira, whom Ifill knew as a child and from his mother Eudora who clearly remembered "Granny Louisa" the budding photographer was able to recreate the story of his ancestry.

From this oral tradition he learnt that Louisa Kettel's owner was Burton Williams after whom Williamsville was named. When news of the abolition of slavery reached remote Williamsville in 1838 the slaves were so overjoyed that they made a "ring-a-roses" around Williams and sang the "Thankee Massa" song. Louisa Kettel had two daughters, namely Kitsy, who was, sadly, murdered in her youth and Sataira who moved to San Fernando in search of better employment opportunities. There she met and married Paul from Tobago and they had two children, Phillip and Eudora. Phillip got a job at Usine Ste Madeleine but on his first day of employment at the sugar factory he was killed in an industrial accident. In San Fernando, Eudora met and married Joseph Ifill with whom she had seven children, the oldest of them being Garnet.

Between 1940 and 1947 Garnet attended the San Fernando E. C. (Anglican) school where he went through the normal courses of reading writing and arithmetic, which all primary students took. In 1948 Joseph Ifill obtained employment as a machinist in the Tate and Lyle sugar factory at Brechin Castle, Caroni. He therefore moved with his family to this new environment where they stayed for some five years before returning to San Fernando. Garnet's sojourn in the sugar belt of central Trinidad determined his life's direction. He became thoroughly fascinated by estate life: the animals on the estate, the alternating of the rolling landscape of Forres Park with the flatness of California, the never-ending round of religious festivities, the yearly cane fires and the efforts by the East Indians to re-create the environment so that it could remind them of the ancestral place.

For the East Indian population, the fifties of the last century was an important transition period. In May of 1845 some 227 of them had first arrived in Port of Spain after one hundred and three days of sailing from Calcutta. In this new *janam bhoomi* (birth place) they sought to re-establish the Bihari heartland from whence most of them had come. This long journey, in its physical and spiritual aspects has always been a subject of tremendous curiosity for Garnet Ifill, ever since, as a youth, he encountered this ever-changing landscape. It is the restoration of that shattered past that forms the theme of this collection. For the descendants of those who toiled and continue to create sugar, rum, molasses and bagasse, this is a useful record of the heritage.

During Garnet's mid-teens at Fonrose Street in San Fernando his dutiful parents tried to make something useful of the lad. They wanted him to become an electrical engineer so they sent him to the San Fernando Technical School; later on he was apprenticed to the Trinidad leaseholds Limited refinery at Pointe-a-Pierre. But he was restless. "The geography of Central Trinidad" as he recalled, had captured him. He wanted to record the movement which was taking place; he wanted to be a photographer.

Fortunately for him, his mother was a woman of great understanding and did not press him in these early endeavours. Instead, she bought him his first camera, a Comflax. He knew little about cameras but he fiddled with the device until it worked. With a functioning camera in hand, the youthful photographer began taking pictures of familiar

San Fernando subjects. His first opportunity to enter the limelight came when he showed some of his to Conrad Bennett, the *Trinidad Guardian* photographer. Bennett liked his work and a job as the Guardian's Southern photographer followed. He had, of course, to use his own equipment and the newspaper undertook to pay only for those pictures which it used. But Garnet Ifill was on his way! He would use this niche to achieve his vision. During 1958 and 1959 he maintained contact with relatives in California eagerly enquiring about study possibilities in the U.S.A. When these contacts assured him of the opportunity to study photography in California, he left Trinidad in 1959.

Life in the U.S.A. and at the Los Angeles Technical College was no bed of roses for this financially strapped youth from San Fernando. He paid his way through college by doing odd jobs in the field of photography. He assisted, for example in the preparation of the work of his fellow students. To his continuous surprise, his own assignments, submitted by him always got lower grades than the work which he did for others. Nevertheless, he utilized his American time profitably. He read widely of the work of the master artists Michelangelo, Picasso and Van Gogh. Under the tutelage of the master fashion photographer Peter Gowland, he learnt the nuances of scene photography namely, lighting, subject, dimension and impact. In 1962, the year of his graduation, he grasped the opportunity to enter the Los Angeles County Fair photography competition. There he won a Silver as well as a Gold medal, much to the delight of his former employers back home. "Ex-Guardian man does the "Impossible"", thundered the *Trinidad Guardian*:

> Mr. Garnet Ifill former Trinidad Guardian photographer was awarded a perfect score of 50 points in the recent Los Angeles County Fair for colour photography.[2]

The article went on to say that Ifill's photographs were published in the magazine of the Los Angeles Trade and Technical College and that Professor Billings, Ifill's instructor

[2] *Trinidad Guardian*. 21 December, 1962. p.16.

had remarked that "never before have I heard of anyone getting a perfect score. This is really an extra-ordinary achievement." During his US sojourn, too, Ifill sought the company of those who had inspired America and had become exemplars to Caribbean youths. In 1961 for example, he met Martin Luther King the energetic, charismatic black civil rights leader.

He held audience with Robert Kennedy, then a rising star in the American political firmament and sought regular counselling from a former Cedros school teacher Mervyn Dymally who also had a dream.

Ifill returned to Trinidad in 1963 and resumed his career as a professional photographer but he still felt that he needed more art in his photography. So he spent long hours, during the mid-sixties, with leading artists such as the late Sonnylal Rambissoon of Mount Stewart Village and Ralph Baney of Phillipine Estate near San Fernando. Baney was at that time, an Art Officer with Trinidad's Ministry of Education (1962-1971) and was himself destined to great things.

By 1976 he graduated with the Ph.D. in Fine Arts at Maryland University and from that year to 1999 when he retired, was Professor of Fine Arts at the Community College of Baltimore County. His paintings and sculpture adorn many homes, public places and

museums in the Americas. On a visit to Trinidad in July of 2002 Dr. Baney vividly recalled the days when the young photographer chatted with him regularly as he sharpened his artistic skills. By the 1970's Ifill had established himself as a photographic artist of superior calibre. His pictures were now being used by *National Geographic*, the *New York Times* and by the Travel Section of London's *Sunday Times*.[1]

The sugar industry became the mainstream of the Caribbean economy since the middle of the seventeenth century when King Sugar replaced a variety of uneconomic crops throughout the region. That sugar revolution was of course, facilitated by the increasing European demand for sugar and its by products as well as by the availability of African slaves cheaply bought off the West African coast. Louisa Kettel's forbears had been transported to Hardbargain in this way. After the Napoleonic Wars had ended in 1815 the British sought to free themselves of the responsibility for African soldiers who had so faithfully fought for them in the preceding wars. As part of their compensation for military service many of these former soldiers were settled at Hardbargain. But many of these men found the place so true to its name-Hardbargain- that they demanded a better location. They were therefore given a New Grant, closer to the larger settlement at

[1] See for example *The Sunday Times*. 6th August, 1989.

Savana Grande (modern Princes Town). Quite possibly Louisa Kettel had interacted with some of these former soldiers.

After 1845 East Indians joined their African brethren on the Williamsville estates continuing the labour-intensive production of sugar, rum, molasses, bagasse and tons of manure which were ploughed back into the fields. They opened up additional fields athwart the existing acres particularly in the Naparimas and in Central Trinidad. To these new openings the East Indians gave names derived from the Gangetic Plains and beyond: Fyzabad, Golkonda, Calcutta Settlement and Kanpur (modern Campo). To them sugar cultivation was not new. Ancient Indian records indicate the presence of *Sakkar Gana* or *Eekh* as a well-known plant, the basis of many beverages and food items in the Indo-Gangetic belt of North India.

As Europe made more and more contact with Asia from the fifteenth century sugar and its by-products were at the top of the list of imports from South Asia. Thus the introduction of Indians to the Caribbean from 1838 (when the first batch went to British Guiana) was a well-calculated move. Such labourers were very familiar with cane production, coming as they did from the Gangetic plain, the ancient heartland of sugar production. They were usually bonded to the plantation for five years and given inducements to re-indenture themselves for an additional term. These inducements were sometimes monetary, sometimes in the form of land, sometimes both land and money. Additionally, in order to achieve government savings on the promised return passage, time-expired Indians were offered land grants in lieu of the return to the ancestral place. Through these inducements, about 75% of the Indians opted to remain in the Caribbean.

From his African ancestors Garnet Ifill learnt about the African contribution to the development of the place and from his mother's close friends-the Meighoos, Allahars and Karmodys- he learnt of the Indian input. All of these considerations were then mixed in the crucible of his fertile imagination to create these memories of the sugar industry. He saw

Left: Meeting Martin Luther King, 1961

the industry and its artefacts with a seeing eye; he understood, he could empathise.

In the pictures which follow, an effort has been made to match the pictures with what might have been the sentiments of the subjects of the photographs. The most frequently used text is the *Ramcharitmanas* written by Sant Tulsidas an early seventeenth century contemporary of William Shakespeare. This text, popularly known as the *Ramayan* is the most widely used source of reference in the Indian diaspora. Why is this so? The geographical centre of the Ramayan story was Ayodhya in Uttar Pradesh, which two centuries after the writing of the Ramayan, became a leading centre for the recruitment of Indian *girmityas* (agreement signers). The flora and fauna as well as the physical features of that place was very familiar to diasporic Indians. These natural features closely resembled those of the Caribbean, Fiji or Mauritius.

The Ramayan story deals with the theme of exile and return which coincided with the Indians' feeling of exile to foreign plantations. And the return of their hero Rama to his former home symbolized their own hope of someday returning to the motherland. Some did; most did not but the hope was always there.

Finally, the Ramayan story deals with the everyday problems of every person at every time: a parent's obligation to his/her children and vice-versa, the abduction of a princess and the relentless striving of her kith and kin to retrieve her, the dangers of high-vaulting ambition and the simple verities of everyday life. Those Indians who did not smuggle copies of this sacred text in their *jahagi bandals* (ship's belongings) brought the *dohas* and *chaupais* (stanzas) in their minds and those who did neither, encouraged the development of a new class of learned men (pundits) who undertook the espousal of the soul-redeeming words which now formed an essential part of their *kathas*, *satsangs* and *yagnas*.

Another source of photographic inspiration in the text derives from the father of Urdu poetry Mirza Ghalib (1797-1868). Whereas Sant Tulsidas was born on the Eastern end of the Bhojpuri heartland, Ghalib was born in Agra on the Western end. His life ended as the transportation of Indians reached a high point in the post-1857 period. To the Muslims who came to the Caribbean, Ghalib was poet laureate. He wrote in the courtly Persian line and metre as Court Poet to the last Mughal Emperor Bahadur Shah but he was equally at home in the new language which had evolved on the Indian sub-continent as Muslim conquerors interacted with a majority Hindu population. That new language, namely Urdu, which combined Hindi, Persian and Arabic became the *lingua franca* of millions of Muslims spread over the major areas of labour recruitment for the colonies. Like a wandering minstrel, Ghalib travelled extensively among the *ryots* (peasant cultivators) expounding his simple aphorisms, so full of symbolism. The other poets chosen in the collection were not known to the labourers who came but they have been chosen because they express sentiments which shaped the world-view of these Orientals.

Rabindranath Tagore, the early twentieth century Bengali poet evokes memories of the same physical and spiritual terrain whence the indentureds came. Subsequent to their ancestors' arrival, Tagore has become the darling of diasporic Indians who relate very intimately with his evocative, even mystical probings into the human spirit. The same can be said of another poet selected for this collection, namely Khalil Gibran (1883-1931). This Lebanese mystic wrote in a touching style which has a special appeal to the Oriental mind. Gibran could take as mundane a matter as buying and selling and invest it with deep symbolic intent as in this piece from *The Prophet*:

> And before you leave the market-place, see that no one has gone away with empty hands, For the master spirit of the earth shall not sleep peacefully upon the wind till the needs of the least of you are satisfied.

The other poets who form the backdrop to these photos are all equally significant: Derek Walcott, Robert Frost and William Shakespeare about whom little needs to be said. How does one gild gold?

In the final analysis, however, Garnet Ifill becomes the centre of this discourse. Here is a Caribbean man who from his boyhood days had a vision of where he wanted to go and like the persistent estate mule, he looked only ahead, surmounting his slender economic means and the absence of those aids which nurture the artist. Derek Walcott, again in his Nobel acceptance speech, reflected on the excuses we make in the Caribbean for lack of creative effort:

> Here there are not enough books, one says, no theatres, no museums, simply not enough to do. Yet, deprived of books, a man must fall back on thought and out of thought, if he can learn to order it, will come the urge to record.[2]

It is in the ordering of that memory, Walcott concludes, that commemoration is achieved. Ifill emerges as a major Caribbean raconteur. This collection is testimony.

The author wishes to acknowledge the assistance of a number of persons who made

[2] *Walcott. P.73.*

this publication possible. Arif Ali shared in the initial excitement which this photographic collection evoked and subsequently suggested additional explanations to the original text. These will, hopefully, make the commentary more comprehensible to a wider audience. Ms. Sherry Ann Singh of our History Department made useful comments on the introduction and suggested many of the captions on the photographs. Vinod Sandlesh of the Indian High Commission in Port of Spain kindly provided the Hindi typing and Ms. Kelly Rumsey of the History Department patiently did the complicated typing of the rest of the work. Above all, Garnet Ifill was a most tolerant interviewee, never tiring of the constant questions. Mrs. Esther Bain-Charles of the Ifill Studio was equally co-operative, despite frequent intrusions into her schedule. This book is dedicated to the memory of Eudora Ifill, a truly remarkable woman, whose firm but caring hand carefully moulded Garnet and his siblings. It is of such people that great civilizations are made. In this particular case, she would be well pleased with her son.

Brinsley Samaroo
History Department
University of the West Indies
St. Augustine
May 2003

Images

PICTURE 1:
A HOME OF OUR OWN
La Fortune, Oropouche. 1972

As soon as they were freed from indentureship the Indians acquired small plots of land near the estate and built their homes in a re-created Indian environment. The windows face the east to catch the breeze, the mango which the Indians introduced to the Caribbean provides leaves to be used in prayer, fruit to be eaten and finally wood to be used in making drums or as fuel. The chickens (murga) and the water tank or "copper" provided food and drink for the family. The copper was used for boiling the syrup, part of the refining process.

PICTURE 2:
THE TRAVELER HAS TO KNOCK AT EVERY ALIEN DOOR TO COME TO HIS OWN
Rabindranath Tagore.
Gitanjali, p.10

Guard's hut at Golconda Crossing in Naparima showing the tracks of the passenger and cane trains to Usine St. Madeleine. The Golconda settlement was first established by indentureds who came from the medieval Mughal fortress city of Golconda in Andhra Pradesh. By the 1920's a thriving village had developed surrounded by lush cane fields and vegetable gardens to supply the San Fernando market. Sugar cane railways were introduced in Trinidad from as early as 1839 preceding the Trinidad government passenger railway which began in 1876. By the early 20th century, standard and narrow gauge engines were purchased for the Caroni and Usine St. Madeleine estates. Most of the locomotives were steam powered but from 1938 diesel engines were added to the locomotive fleet. The manufacturers of this rolling stock were British engineering companies. In 1997 the transportation of canes by trains ended, closing a long and exciting era of sugar cane rail transport.

PICTURE 3:

BELI BITAP SAB SAPHALA
SAPHOOLA.
THE TREES AND CREEPERS
WERE ALL LADEN WITH
FRUITS AND BLOSSOMS
Ramcharitmanas. Des.II. 278. 2

Fruit, leaves and flowers have traditionally been sacred to Indians. For this reason they sought to bless their intended Caribbean homes with seeds and cuttings hidden in their *jahagi bandals* (ship's belongings): mangoes, pomme-granate, guava, tamarind, dhalls (pulses), bhagis (spinach), neem, behl, thyme, cowah and pomme-arac. These have complemented the flora and fauna which was native to the Caribbean, adding richness and variety to the region. Cane arrows welcome the harvesters to reap the profitable cane at the Phillipine estate to the South of San Fernando. This estate was one of the earliest to be set up, during the period of African slavery which ended in 1838. From 1845 Indians were brought here to complement the work force since many Africans moved away from estate work. After indentureship, the Indians remained on or close to the estates now adding their caste-derived skills to the labour force. In this way whole cadres of specialized skills developed: sonar (jewellers), darzi (tailors), lohars (blacksmiths), gualbance and ahirs (cattle-minders), julahas (weavers) and kumhars (ceramic artists).

PICTURE 4:
*YOUR HOUSE IS YOUR
LARGER BODY: IT GROWS
IN THE SUN AND SLEEPS
IN THE STILLNESS; AND IT
IS NOT DREAMLESS. DOES
NOT YOUR HOUSE
DREAM? AND DREAMING
LEAVE THE CITY FOR
GROVE OR HILLTOP?*
Kahlil Gibran The Prophet. 38

This 1968 picture of a house in
Gopee Trace, Penal could have
been taken anywhere in Bihar.
The thatched roof, the open
kitchen and the cane fields in
the background all remind of
another, ancestral place

PICTURE 5:
SO SABU SAHIYA JO DAI-U SAHAAWA.
WE MUST BEAR ALL THAT FATE IMPOSES ON US.
Ramcharitmanas. Des. II. 245.3.

Children were often kept home to assist at crop-time. The buffalo was one of the early imports from India and was used, even up to the 1970's to transport the canes from the fields to the cane railway stations from whence the canes were taken to the sugar factory. Rochard Douglas Scale yard. 1972

PICTURE 6:
LOADING THE SCALES AT ROCHARD DOUGLAS. 1972

The bundles of freshly-cut cane are weighed and loaded on to trailer carriages to be taken to the Usine. When the Indians were brought to the Caribbean, to work on the sugar estates, they came to an occupation which they had known from the ancient times. Vedic sources speak of the sweet plant "sakkar jana" from which the holy men made "soma" to assist in their meditations. From India, Arab traders took the plants to the Iberian Peninsula where, with early African slavery, sugar was produced on the offshore islands owned by the Portuguese. At the start of the 16th century Nicholas de Ovando introduced the plant to Hispaniola. At the same time, the Portuguese took the plant to their colony in Brazil. It was from Brazil, during the mid-17th century that sugar canes took root in the British and French colonies.

PICTURE 7:
*MY HOME WOULD HAVE
BEEN DESOLATE, EVEN
WITHOUT MY TEARS*
Ghalib

An overseer's (sirdar) house at Brechin Castle, Caroni in 1970. The house is on the edge of the cane field and is built of clay bricks. Note the slatted "Demerara windows" built to block the rain but to allow the breeze to filter through. These windows were imported from British Guiana where they were invented to catch the sea breeze on the coastal plains, home to the majority of the population. Guyanese hardwoods, used in the making of the slats, could be relied upon for many years.

PICTURE 8:
KYK-OVER-AL (SEE EVERYTHING)

The early Dutch presence in the Guayanas, so close to Trinidad, resulted in the transference of land reclamation methods to Trinidad and, of course, appropriate names to managers' residences. Manager's House at Picton Estate. South Naparima during the 1960's.

PICTURE 9:

THIS LAND WAS OURS BEFORE WE WERE THE LAND'S. SHE WAS OUR LAND MORE THAN A HUNDRED YEARS BEFORE WE WERE HER PEOPLE.
Robert Frost. *In the clearing.* New York. 1962. p 31.

The *bhaisa* or water buffalo was one of the early 19th century importations from India to work on the sugar plantations. Originally bred in the swampy areas of the lower Gangetic plains they developed an early adaptation to harsh climatic conditions. In the Caribbean, they were essential for bringing the heavy sugar cane carts from muddy, trackless fields to the more accessible stations. These sturdy animals were also very useful in other agricultural occupations such as rice and vegetable cultivation and in the logging industry. From the 1970's they were genetically engineered to produce the buffalo from the land of the calypso – the buffalypso. These Brechin Castle buffalypsoes formed the core of a prize herd of animals now used as beef and milk producers. They have been exported to the United States and Northern South America where they continue to be profitably produced.

PICTURE 10:
ORIAHI HATH, ASANIHU KE GHAE. IT IS BY ONE'S OWN ARMS ALONE THAT ONE PARRIES THE STRIKES EVEN OF A THUNDERBOLT. Ramcharitmanas. Des. II 305.4

The burden of plantation labour fell equally on women as upon men. But their wages were lower. This sugar worker at Woodford Lodge Estate in Caroni, had to wake up at four in the morning, prepare breakfast for her family and then take up work at around six. Dressed to guard against the sharp leaves and pointed sugar cane stalks as well as to ward off a multitude of insects, she must make her daily quota if she is to be paid. After toiling in the hot sun until the early afternoon she would go home to continue her labours: cooking, washing and cleaning for tomorrow's new beginning.

PICTURE 11:
PAAVAN SUNDAR SUDHAA SAMANA.
PURE, LOVELY AND DELICIOUS AS AMBROSIA.
Ramcharitmanas. Des. II 278.4

Every Caribbean country lad is familiar with the sweet saccharine flavour of freshly cut, teeth peeled sugar cane. This well-ventilated son of a sugar worker at Forres Park Estate knows how to supplement his diet!

PICTURE 12:
*TO YOU THE EARTH
YIELDS HER FRUIT, AND
YOU SHALL NOT WANT IF
YOU BUT KNOW HOW TO
FILL YOUR HANDS.*
Gibran. The Prophet. p 44

Rochard Road Scale Yard in Barrackpore has always been a focal point for the sugar industry. On this busy day in 1986 many farmers have brought their canes to filled in the long carriages in the background. Notice the galvanized buckets on the carts, to water the buffaloes in the heated afternoon sun.

PICTURE 13:
TO LOVE LIFE THROUGH LABOUR IS TO BE INTIMATE WITH LIFE'S INMOST SECRET.
Gibran. p 33

On Union Estate, just outside San Fernando, this 1968 Ifill photograph captures a woman's efforts to save a field that has been burnt. Cane fields were burnt during periods of dispute between workers and management, mostly over wages and working conditions. Sometimes fires would be started because of the careless dropping of a cigarette butt or the spread of a bush fire in the dry season. If the cane is not quickly cut after burning it looses its sucrose content and is rendered useless. Clearing a burnt field meant longer, more incessant hours of work.

PICTURE 14:
OWA TANA SIAM.
MULES ON THEIR OFF-DAY
AT BRONTE ESTATE, NEAR
SAN FERNANDO IN 1967.

They rolled in the dust to work out their tiredness and to coat their bodies with insect-repelling dust and dung. Because of the pressing need for transport in the sugar industry, mules supplemented buffalo labour, carrying fertilizer, cane cuttings for planting and for fodder, tools and equipment as well as loads of sugar canes in crop-time. They were hardy, easy to maintain but stubborn when overloaded.

PICTURE 15:
NOR, WHEN THEIR DESTIN'D LABOUR IS PERFORMED, BE THOU ASHAMED TO LEAD THE PANTING MULES TO THE WARM PEN; WHERE COPIOUS FORAGE STROWED. AND STRENUOUS RUBBING, RENOVATE THEIR STRENGTH SO FEWER AILS (ALAS! HOW PRONE TO AILS!). THEIR DAYS SHALL SHORTEN; AH, TOO SHORT AT BEST.
Dr. James Grainger. *The Sugar Cane: a poem in four books.* London. 1764. p 101.

Before the importation of the buffalo and zebu bull from India in the 19th century, it was the highly prized mule which did most of the heavy field transportation. In this 1967 photo, the mules have just completed their day's work in the crop time.

PICTURE 16:
I AM SO COOPED UP IN TIME AND SPACE, I CANNOT EVEN SHED TEARS ENOUGH.
Ghalib.

The Usine Ste. Madeleine estate in the Naparimas was one of the largest on the island. Here, Indians replaced Africans from the 1840's, even being housed in cottages vacated by Africans. As these cottages fell to ruin, they were replaced by estate barracks which, like this one, crowded four to six families in one shed-like building, with little privacy and few basic amenities. Barrack life often became synonymous with alcoholism, spousal abuse and petty quarrels. The occupants longed for the day when they could escape barrack-life.

PICTURE 17:
*BHAE BIDHI BIMUKH
BIMUKH SABU KOU.
WHEN FATE IS ADVERSE
EVERYONE ELSE TURNS
HOSTILE.*
Ramcharitmanas Des II. 181.1.

Barrack life was a crowded existence yet the Indians sought to re-create a familiar environment. The mango tree on the right and the bamboo poles, to be used for making a tent for impending prayers, joined with the ever-present dog to create a scene of uneasy rural peace.

PICTURE 18:
WAITING FOR ASHFORD

In 1958 Ashford Sinanan, a prominent member of the Democratic Labour Party was eagerly contesting for ascendancy in elections to the federal parliament of the West Indian federation. As he journeyed by train from San Fernando to Ben Lomond, supporters in the sugar belt waited with eager expectancy for his arrival. Although Ifill is standing in front of the line of men, no eyes are turned to him; everyone is waiting for Ashford!

PICTURE 19:
*STE. MADELEINE SUGAR
FACTORY DURING THE
1960'S*

This sugar factory, established in the late 19th century, became the major centre for sugar operations in the South. Its huge chimney was a beacon for many miles around and the sweet smell of grinding cane was wafted to the adjoining roadways, making that passage a pleasant experience. It was to this factory that canes came from Barrackpore and Bronte, Golconda and Picton, Union and La Fortune.

PICTURE 20:
NIYATAM KURU KARMA
TVAM KARMA JYAAYO HY
AKAR MANAH.
DO THY ALLOTTED WORK,
FOR ACTION IS BETTER
THAN INACTION.
Bhagavadgita. Ch.3. V.8

Crop time on Union Estate near San Fernando was a busy time, when man and mule provided companionship to each other. In the foreground the mules wait to be loaded, in the background they are moving away towards the Scale Yard to be weighed and loaded for dispatch to Usine.

PICTURE 21:

UTSEEDIYUR IME LOKAA
NA KURYAAM KARMA CED,
AHAM SAMKARASYA CA,
KARTAA SYAAM UPAHAN
YAAM IMAAH PRAJAAH.
IF I SHOULD CEASE WORK,
THESE FIELDS WOULD
FALL IN RUIN AND I
SHOULD BE THE CREATOR
OF DISORDERED LIFE AND
DESTROY THESE PEOPLE.
Bhagavadgita. Ch.3. V.24.

Debe in the dry season of 1973. The Indians devised an all-year system of cultivation. The canes are planted in the rainy season and reaped at the start of the dry season some 12 months afterwards. After the crop-time reaping of the canes they planted vegetables on the adjoining lands. The low-lying lands in the background would be blossoming fields of bodi, watermelon, karailli, bhagi and bhaigan. These would provide income and food after the canes have been sold.

PICTURE 22:
NIJ KAR GRIHA PARICHARJAA KARAEE. SHE DID ALL THE HOUSEHOLD WORK WITH HER OWN HANDS.
Ramcharitmanas. Des. VII. 23.3.

After completing her days work on the Ben Lomond estate, Rupanee returns to the old barrack building where her ancestors had lived, to prepare the evening meal and "tidy-up the place" for her family's return. She smiles in anticipation of that re-union, as she "manjays" (cleans) the "bartan" (kitchen utensils).

PICTURE 23:
THE HOUSE REFLECTS THE QUALITY OF HIM WHO IN IT DWELLS.
Ghalib.

This mud hut (ajoupa) with walls of gobar (cow dung) mixed with earth, covered with carat leaves gathered from the adjacent forest, provided shelter and shade for a Barrackpore family. The name Barrackpore was brought from the soldiers' garrison just north of Calcutta called Barrack-pur (town of soldiers) from which many indentured labourers had come. Here in Barrackpore they re-built the dwellings which they had abandoned in Barrack-pur.

PICTURE 24:
*A GATHERING OF
BARRACKPORE MULES
(1957)*

The day's work is over and the
mules bond with each other in
the evening breeze. But they
cannot wander around as they
please. Vishnu keeps them in his
view as his sturdy mount frames
the herd.

PICTURE 25:
BLACKSMITH,
BLACKSMITH MAKE ME A
SHOE!

A mule patiently waits to be fitted up at the estate blacksmith's shop. It is the dry season and the canes on the hill beyond are waiting to be harvested. Bronte Estate. 1966. It was the blacksmith who carefully crafted the estate carts, with a 12 foot shaft of a horse, a 10 foot for a mule and a 14 foot shaft for a buffalo cart.

PICTURE 26:
*SASI SAMPANNA SOHA
MAHI KAISEE, UPKAREE
KAI SAMPATI JAISEE.
THE EARTH, RICH WITH
CROPS APPEARS AS
DELIGHTFUL AS THE
WEALTH OF A GENEROUS
MAN.*
Ramcharitmanas. Des. IV. 14.2

Carter-men were very important on the estate. They and their mules provided the essential link between the fields and scale-yard, trudging through roadless areas, crossing ravines and tall grass bringing the precious canes within reach of transport and factory. Union Estate. 1966.

PICTURE 27
PICTURE 28
PHERAHI CHATUR TURAG
GATI NAANAA.
THE CLEVER FELLOWS
PUT THEIR STEEDS
THROUGH VARIOUS
PACES.
Ramcharitmanas. Des. I. 298.1

Crop-over ceremonies formed part of every estate's ritual. Picton Estate in 1956 was no exception. In these two pictures of the Picton crop-over fete a black overseer rides a white horse and a white overseer rides a black horse.

PICTURE 29:
PRABHU KEE KRIPA
BHAYAU SABU KAAJOO.
EVERYTHING HAS TURNED
OUT WELL BY THE GRACE
OF THE LORD!
Ramcharitmanas. Des. V. 29.2

By the early 1970's tractors increasingly replaced the mule, buffalo and bullock carts which had done yeoman service for over a century. Tractors, manufactured mainly in the United Kingdom, became the preferred means of transport.

PICTURE 30:
EHI TE MOR KAAHA AB
NEEKAA
I CANNOT EXPECT
GREATER GOOD THAN
THIS AT PRESENT.
Ramcharitmanas. Des. II. 179.3

From mud huts in Bihar, the sugar workers transferred to mud huts in Barrackpore but Trinidad offered possibilities for upward mobility which were not available in Bihar. From the fifties of the last century, they were able to accumulate sufficiently to build sturdy homes such as this one at Rochard Junction with the residence on the upper floor and a bar and a grocery beneath. From these humble beginnings there arose a whole generation of professionals, many migrating to North America, continuing that never-ending odyssey from continent to continent, which had started from Calcutta in February of 1845.

PICTURE 31:
THE CARTER MAN HOMEWARD PLODS HIS WEARY WAY AND LEAVES THE WORLD TO DARKNESS AND TO ME.
Forres Park Estate. 1968

The carter man is making his last trip for the day; the car tyres replacing the heavy wood-and-iron cartwheel was his contribution to innovation and certainly makes the pulling easier.

PICTURE 32:
CHARHI CHARHI RATH
BAAHER NAGAR, LAAGEE
JURAN BARAAT.
MOUNTING CHARIOTS,
THE PROCESSIONISTS
BEGIN TO COLLECT
OUTSIDE THE TOWN.
Ramcharitmanas. Des. I. 299.

At Palmiste estate, owned in the 19th century by Sir Norman Lamont and his family, crop-over ceremonies were popular. In this picture the muleteers have mounted their "Chariots" and are ready to roll! Notice the original estate cartwheel, with 12 spokes of balata wood crafted on to an axle made of locust wood. The design had come from India.

PICTURE 33:
JOW BINU AVASAR ATHAVA DINESOO, JAG KEHI KAHAHU NA HOI KALESOO.
IF THE SUN SETS BEFORE TIME, WHO IN THIS WORLD WILL NOT BE SUBJECTED TO HARDSHIP?
Ramcharitmanas. Des. II. 304.4

In this picture four women on the Forres Park Estate cut canes to supply one carter man. The field on the opposite side of the road has been cut but this field has been burnt. It has to be reaped quickly.

PICTURE 34:
*INVOKE THE MASTER
SPIRIT OF THE EARTH, TO
COME INTO YOUR MIDST
AND SANCTIFY THE
SCALES AND THE
RECKONING THAT WEIGHS
AGAINST VALUE.*
Gibran. 44.

Whilst the mules wait patiently, the cane is weighed and lifted on the waiting carriages of a "Caroni Ltd." Transport train. This is a typical plantation picture and could have been taken in Fiji or Mauritius, South Africa or Guyana. The plantation system was a great unifier, creating a bondage that invisibly joined thousands of Indians in common labour.

PICTURE 35:
WHILE SUCH FAIR SCENES ADORN THESE BLISSFUL ISLES, WHY WILL THEIR SONS, UNGRATEFUL, ROAM ABROAD? WHY SPEND THEIR OPULENCE IN OTHER CLIMES?
Dr. J. Grainger *The Sugar Cane*. 1764. p 118

Whether it was 1764 or 1954, the sugar plantations of the Caribbean always attracted young English, Scottish and Irishmen. Here the young overseers and managers, attended by their local grooms, gather for the Picton Estate gymkhana.

PICTURE 36:
JAHA TAHA PIAHI BIBIDH MRIG NEERAA.
BEASTS OF VARIOUS KINDS DRANK OF ITS WATER WHENEVER THEY LISTED.
Ramcharitmanas. Des. III. 38.4

In this 1954 snapshot of mules drinking from a common "copper" the sweat on the animals' haunches make them glisten in the sun. The estate is Brechin Castle in Caroni. The respite will be short! The field in the background has to be cleared.

PICTURE 37:
ONCE MORE, INTO THE BREACH DEAR FRIENDS!

Sugar canes being unloaded from the carriages into the grinders at Brechin Castle. By the 1950's steam-driven cranes were in full use hastening the movement of the brown gold, producing fine crystals so popular on the world market.

PICTURE 38:
*GIVE US THIS DAY OUR
DAILY BREAD*

Four sugar workers at Forres
Park pause to give thanks for
their shared lunch, on a freshly
cut field. The mule waits
patiently with his load in the
background whilst the metal
"food carrier" sits next to its
owner. This lunch is no picnic,
it is eaten under the boiling
sun in the allotted lunch hour.
The afternoon shift will now
commence!

PICTURE 39:
YET UNLESS THE EXCHANGE BE IN LOVE AND KINDLY JUSTICE, IT WILL BUT LEAD SOME TO GREED AND OTHERS TO HUNGER
Gibran. 44

Cane being lifted to the train in Debe in1955. Here again the steam boiler is being used to make the haulage more efficient.

PICTURE 40:
SANTI HRIDAYA JASA
NIRMAL BAAREE.
ITS WATER WAS AS LIMPID
AS THE HEART OF SAINTS.
Ramcharitmanas. Des. III. 38.4

In 1955 the cooling system at Usine Ste. Madeleine was still new. The cooling towers on the left ensured a constant flow of fresh water from the large Usine pond in the foreground. The main chimney towers to the right whilst the Palmiste palms in the far background assisted in the recreation of a familiar Bihari landscape. The Usine pond doubled up as a recreation centre, easing the drudgery of plantation labour.

PICTURE 41:
NIDARI PAVANU JANU
CHAHATA URAANE.
THEY WOULD FLY IN THE
AIR, AS IT WERE,
OUTSTRIPPING THE WIND
ITSELF.
Ramcharitmanas. Des. I. 297.3

Indians on the estates sought to enact the scenes from their sacred scriptures which told of wars and tournaments, displays of strength and acts of graciousness. Whenever the chance arose, as again at Picton Estate, they sought public acclamation through acts of daring as this effort to tame a bucking bronco. The assembled crowd is obviously enjoying the spectacle.

PICTURE 42:

PICTURE 43:
*WE HAVE NO TIME TO
LOSE, AND HAVING NO
TIME WE MUST SCRAMBLE
FOR OUR CHANCES. WE
ARE TOO POOR TO BE
LATE.*
Tagore, 76.

Garnet Ifill was particularly fond of Forres Park Estate, near Claxton Bay, because of its undulating nature, with hills and hollows, to create perspective and depth to his photographic creations. Here the men ride and the women walk, each wending their separate ways. It was from their labour that Caroni's world famous "Forres Park" rum was created from the forties. A full and potent blend, Forres Park Rum was the ancestor of later popular blends such as "Stallion" and "White Magic Light".

PICTURE 44:
OLD AGE IS A
CONFLAGRATION. AS
FIERCE AS THE CANE
FIRES OF CROP TIME I
WILL PASS THROUGH
THESE PEOPLE LIKE A
CLOUD.
Derek Walcott: The Saddhu of
Couva. 1979

Having served his indentures,
Aja finds comfort among the
jhandis (flags) of La Fortune
Estate. With cane in hand and
hobbled gait he threads the
village street, respected by all
for his years of honest labour.
What will be his reward? No
pension surely but the hope
that soon he will be re-born to
a higher destiny – a just
reward for karma.

PICTURE 45:
TREE AT MY WINDOW, WINDOW TREE. MY SASH IS LOWERED WHEN NIGHT COMES ON; BUT LET THERE NEVER BE CURTAIN DRAWN BETWEEN YOU AND ME.
Collected poems of Robert Frost. New York. 1936. p 318

With a canopy of trees around, this cane farmer's dwelling in Cottage Estate, South Naparima was home enough. On lots purchased on abandoned sugar lands the workers created their own spaces, abutting on the road, with a vegetable garden at the back. In this way they nurtured successive generations of Caribbean people.

PICTURE 46:
KADALI TAAL BAR DHUJAA PATAAKAA.
THE STATELY PALMS ARE STANDING LIKE BEAUTIFUL PENNONS AND STANDARDS.
Ramcharitmanas. Des. III. 37.1

Brechin Castle, Caroni, factory in 2000. Slated for demolition as the sugar industry is being quietly phased out, this intimacy between the raw material and the final products – the cane and the factory – will soon be only a memory

PICTURE 47:
'MONG SALTS ESSENTIAL,
SUGAR WINS THE PALM.
FOR TASTE, FOR COLOUR
AND FOR VARIOUS USE.
AND IN THE NECTAR OF
THE YELLOWEST CANE
MUCH ACOR, OIL AND
MUCILAGE ABOUND.
Dr. James Grainger *The Sugar Cane* 1764. p 105

This golden, brown heap of sweet-smelling Brechin Castle sugar waits in the warehouse to be shipped to the United Kingdom. There it will be sold as brown sugar or converted into a variety of bye-products.